DEEP IN THE BOWELS OF GOTHAM

Poems

2003 – 2013

Theresa Marie Reel

Dedicated to The New Woodhaven Poetry Workshop

and

The Gotham Writers Workshop

Thank you for expanding my vision

TABLE OF CONTENTS

What Care I

If my lover sings me lullabies---
What care I for passers-by?

If my lover be young—or old---
What care I for the heat or the cold?

If my lover's eyes be blue . . . or brown---
What care I if stocks are sound?

If my lover is full of fun---
What care I for the State of the Union?

And if my lover's voice is soft and deep---
Then, what care I when the world weeps?

This, Then, Must Be My Rest

This, then, must be my rest---
as I sit in quiet stillness
listening to the din in my mind
play back what I should have said to you.

This, then, must be my rest---
to lay with a book
but long for your body
beside mine;
to listen to music
and cry for thoughts of you.

This, then, must be my rest---
to hurry through my workday
carrying the weight of my resentment
at your absence.

This, then, must be my rest---
to toss and turn in my soft bed
with sad, sad dreams of you.

I Own It

My sadness---
My darkness---
I own it.

It is mine
until the
day I die;

and if there
is another life
to come,

I will carry it
with me
into Hell.

Mirror Check

Do I have snakes in my hair?
Someone, please tell me.

Do I have fangs,
or claws?

Do I have a tail growing out of my
backside?

Call me, damn it---
Come to me---
and kiss me madly---

or soon you *will* see
snakes and fangs and
claws and an
angry, twitching
tail.

Self Portrait as a Hurricane

Exasperation fuels the winds---
Tears give rise to raindrops---
Harsh words and anger swirl around
the circle of an eye,
like loud sea gulls trapped in a small room.
My path is charted.
I burst out of the semi-tropics
gathering furniture and clothes and the cat---
I blow out of Mississippi---
I crash into New York City.

On Viewing a Civil War Photo

General Sherman said, "War isn't a tea party."
There is no glamor in mud and blood---
No beauty in torn limbs
or cannon cratered landscapes---
the sounds of war are unlike
those of the clink of fine china and sliver.
Sweat encrusted uniforms don't feel like silk and lace.
Gunpowder and tobacco dominate
the scent of dogwood and honeysuckle.
And the taste of death
will never be the taste of tea cakes.
So what Truth is there in war?
Only that young men who are loved
become but cadavers that will rot away
into the sucking mud.

Light

Light is illumination;
it is a fiery angel;
it is the comet's fall from Heaven;
it is the knowledge of the forbidden---
exposing the unseen---
it opens dark corners where
roaches and demons hide.
It is a particle
but is also a wave
a wave of particles that penetrate---
a wave of particles that expose the Universe.

How to be a Loose Woman

Oddly enough, your clothes must be tight---
You must laugh loudly and with your heart.
 Flirt with the Devil;
 Don't look both ways before crossing the street---
 Bound and bounce across the boulevard.
 Don't make your bed;
 Gargle with bourbon;
 Eat chocolate for breakfast;
 Take long bubble baths
  that use up *all* the hot water;
 Be alert for opportunities to provoke;
 Wear stockings;
 Stomp hard with those heels as you roam at large;
 Kiss the men and make them cry . . .
  and moan;
  Dance like a woman possessed.
 The Baptists will rub your name from the
 Book of Heaven---
 but what of it?
 Yours is the here and the now.

The Dream

St. Magdeline's Eve
is the night
of Love dreams.
Fortune is supposed
to send you a dream
of the One for you.
So before I go to bed
I ask for a dream---
I beg for a dream---
I demand a dream
that will not come.
Does this mean
Love will never come to me?

I loved someone once
but he died
so it didn't count.

I loved someone once
but he died
and was buried up on the mount.

An old hag sits
in the corner of my room
screeching an eerie warning.
I am afraid to get out of bed
lest she tell me what

I already suspect:
It is easier to chew glass
than to know what Love wants.

A Roma con artist
sits on Jamaica Avenue
and asks
"Would you like a reading, sweetie?"
I rush by
and try to ignore her.

I don't need my Fortune read.
A gift is still a gift
and
ashes are still ashes.

Slowly, and Not Always Dependably

Slowly, and not always dependably---
  but what would we do without it?
  (We might all die)
The boys I grew up with became gauche and rude
  and then they all settled down---
  they all lived in town---
  some of them have died.
They never listened to me---
I am not their mistress---
You are not their master.
The water they drank was as warm as blood
  but there was one who drank it cold.
My memory of him
  consists of his actions---
  not his words.
His gestures of kindness were concrete---
His words, too soft to remember.
Now that he is gone
  who will take his place?
My father always gave me directions---
  and they were always correct
  though I never would believe it at the time.
Now that he is gone
  who will take his place?
I come from the mountains---
But my heart belongs to the sea.
My stories come from my father's knee.
I left the door open for the cat

Although it lets the demons enter,
he will cry all night
if he can't come in.

Last Tango

(on listening to *The Assassin's Tango,* by John Powell)

My sweet love.
Move with me;
twist with me
across the dirt.

My sweet.
Life is sad
but worth holding onto.

Here It comes.
Twist and turn
with me.
Here.
There.
Follow my lead and
I will lead you into
eternal Bliss.

Ignore It's approach---
the pounding steps---
the cold breeze---
Ignore the black night---
the smell of rotting leaves---

Look into my eyes
and believe . . .
Here!
Into my eyes
and
nowhere else---

believe in me only---
or It will get you.

The Beginning of the Modern

Diana's arrows shoot towards the moon---
Through the breezes they sail---
Through the dreams of our night
Screeches the cry of an owl.
Snakes carry the message to the Underworld;
The hearts there beat in dread.
The confused hands of ghosts
Wipe the honey from their lips.
Their cries surge up to the living.
The ancient world is dying.
The secrets of the Mysteries are gone;
The words of the Sybil have no more meaning;
The daemon has been weakened by salt;
The Graces no longer sing.

Last Night I Dreamt

Last night I dreamt you were my father
finally come home from a long, long trip.
You cradled me in your arms---front to back
and I noticed a tattoo on your arm.
You held your mouth against my ear and told
me unfatherly things, but did I mind?

It was enough to have you hold me,
squeezing my ripeness for your enjoyment.
My knees buckled from the weight of delight,
as you, my faux father, and I, your love,
give in---such is how cold medicine works.
Maybe it means something, but probably not.

It's The Same Story

It's the same story---
a story of
queens and adventuresses---
of harlots and glamorous beauties.
These are the stories
that have been told
and are still told to this day.
The Octavias and Elaines
wait
ever constant---
ever alone.
Let this be the point
in the storyline---
where you,
my Hero,
turn from the
exotic and captivating
and turn back . . .
turn around . . .
and return
Home
to me.

Give Us Time

Give us time—
Time to burn each second
upon a piece of paper—
upon unpracticed ears
each second counting down
to the dreaded End

Take all the filled papers
that have been marked by Time
toss them up and watch
them fall down
as we have wasted each second

this is the sorry End

we drown in words up to our ears

Ode

I sing this song in praise of men---
  Men's men---
  Macho men---
Men who work hard
  without complaint
  at soul sucking
  but "good" jobs to support their families---
Men who do what it takes---
Men who want to protect their wives
  and discipline their children.

I sing this song in praise of their Otherness---
  Their voices deep with assurance---
  Their steady eyes---
  Their noses that carry the weight of gravitas
  across the bridge---
  Their jaw lines, like cliffs to be scaled---
  Their strong, hairy arms---
  Their capable hands---
  Their practiced grip---
  Their wide, solid chests---
  Their feet that are anchored to the ground.

I sing of their flavor---
  of earth and sweat and testosterone---
I sing of their smell---
  of Old Spice or cherry tobacco or warm beer.
I sing of how their minds work
  in spectacularly strange ways---
  of how the circuits and pathways
  upon which alien thoughts travel
  constantly surprise---
  as when they cannot hear what you say
  until they have had their morning coffee,
  or when an innocent breath on an earlobe
  turns them all randy.
I could sing of them forever---
    the how and the what and the why of them---
    without ever understanding.
And even though they don't always call when
    they should---
I sing this song in praise of men.

How to Say Goodbye in the Moonlight

Be careful---
it's bad form
to step on
someone's grave.

You may touch
him lightly,
but do not cling---
it only makes things
worse than they
already are.

He leaves
in the darkness;
but the darkness
is your friend too---

Shadows
hide
your tears.

Now,
somewhere
between

this moment
and the rising sun---

Let go.

Five Ways of Looking at the J Train

I

A slow brown slug,
the J makes me
late for work---
I want to step on the gas
but can't.

II

Germs and viruses
cover the poles
as they travel back and forth
across the city.

III

A halfway house
for the homeless and
the disturbed—
riders give alms or
pretend to be asleep.

IV

Roller coaster rides
for children
who sit with their
feet on the seats
as they gaze out
the windows---
"Mommy look
at the rat!"

V

The view from the bridge
is breathtaking---
golden light reflects
off the water---
silver lights glow
from the skyline---
Nature gives hope
to Civilization.

Deep in the Bowels of Gotham

Deep in the bowels of Gotham
the Masters of the Universe fret.
No longer will a dead ram
appease hungry gods---now the gods Net
Worth and Profit both clamor
for stock points and the ring of a bell.
Retrace their steps til they blur
and see how a shiny bronze knife fell
El's bull in Jericho's streets
or how fair flowers and blood mingled
in Joy at Inanna's feet
as all of Nippur was slowly lulled
to sleep. May this city learn to cry---
for it, too, will Blaze and die.

I Know a Lot of Dead Men

I know a lot of dead men---
Sometimes they visit me at night
  and tell tales.

Yet I still blame them---
for their recklessness and their despair.
Many a night they brought joy and happiness
only to abandon me at dawn.

I know a lot of dead men---
Sometimes they visit me at night
  and leave regret.

To Emily

She drifted by in white---
an image in the hall;
leaving messages so slight---
they might mean nothing at all.

Then through the cracks, Light seeps
and slowly, to my delight,
the message rises in Height
before descending Deep.

The Life I Live Now

The life I live now
is dim;
the neon lights
try their best
to light the way,
but fail.
My dreams are
poorly lit
scenes of an
off-kilter city---
the moody
lighting
just heightens
the tension.
Streets are deserted;
My apartment is empty of life;
 A feeling of dread
 sweeps over me
 and I suddenly realize
 I am missing
 parts of myself.
 I search the deep
 dark concrete
 tunnels.
 I join the waiting crowds
 and I know

I will get on
the wrong
train.
How will I survive
the struggle
to find
my way
back?

Two Poems by Louie

(my cat)

Where the Hell Were You

Where the hell were you?
You left me all alone
for 3 ½ whole days.
You dumped me
with an old lady
who reeked of nicotine.
Where the hell were you?
You weren't here to feed me;
You weren't here to clean my litter box.
You weren't here to play with me
and give me sweet smooches
and tell me how handsome and funny I am.
Where the hell were you?
Don't you dare ever do that to me again

Vet Visit

I don't like the smell of this place---
it smells like chemicals and yucky medicine.
Let's get outta here---
Take me home.
I don't like how the air tastes-

it tastes like shih tuz.
Let's get outta here---
Take me home.
I don't like the sounds here---
all the barking and howling
and screeching.
Let's get outta here---
Take me home.
I don't like what I see---
cages full of other cats
(not as special as me)
I don't like this place.
Let's get outta here.
Take me home.
I don't like these hands on me---
They aren't yours and
they are holding a needle.
Let's get outta here---
Take me home.
Take me home right now
or I will do something
so embarrassing
you will never be able
to come here again.

Revelation

The Seekers are weak
from their fast;
they have drunk
of the barley and thyme
kykeon.

At first they are unsure
of what they are seeing---
but then they know
from the smell
of the body on the pyre.
The smell is almost all
that is left.
The Guides will soon
gather the ashes
as the Seekers ask themselves
What is the purpose?

Guides: By this action, Life is made.

The Seekers
do not understand.
At midnight
they carry sheaves
of grain
into the temple
that seems like a cave.

They are unsure.
They clutch the sheaves
to their breasts.
Cold, damp stone
presses them in
before they are led into
the large chamber.

Guides: This is your body.
         It is the ancestor whom you were when
         during your former existence
         you lived.
         Then you went down
         to the sacred mother
         to rest.
         Do you remember?
         Try to remember . . .

The Seekers are led
further into the darkness.

Guides: These are the things worthy to be known.
         Pay attention.

The Guides hold a chest.
The Guides hold a basket.

The Seekers take a marble rod
from the chest.
The Seekers take a bronze krater

from the basket.
The rod goes into
the krater.
Wheat berries
become
powder
like the ash
from the funeral pyre.

Guides: By this action Life is made.
            By this action you create Life.

A woman
dressed in white
and wearing
a crown of wheat
carries a flaming torch
and cries
with all her heart,

Kore! Kore!

Her pain and grief
expand
throughout
the crowd of Seekers.
They follow this frantic woman
wandering in the darkness.

They follow haltingly---

into the Unknown---
into black Coldness---
they clutch their sheaves
and try not to cry out
in fear
from the wild and anguished
screams
that fill their ears.

For the woman
is wild with grief.
They follow her
as she wanders
the Darkness
becoming more and more
agitated.
Where is her daughter?
Where is Kore?
Will they ever find her?
Will they ever see light again?

They become dizzy and lost
amid the columns

Finally
it is barely dawn---
She as yet
barely blushes
in the horizon.

The Seekers know this

because
the woman has led
them into a meadow
lit by hundreds of torches.

Their eyes blink
wearily
in the light.

A Guide's face
greets
the new sky.

Hye!

The Guide
looks down at
the damp earth.

Kye!

The Seekers
also
command,
Kye!

The Guides take the sheaves
from them---
and they feel naked.

The Guides take the sheaves
and place them on a pile nearby.

The Seekers have nothing
to clutch at---
nothing to hold onto.

Guides: Behold, Holy Mother has given birth
to the Powerful One.

A Guide strikes
a bronze gong.

Guide: I call Kore!

Another Guide
sprinkles the ashes
of the dead
on the pile of sheaves.

Guide: By this action, Life is made.

Suddenly
a young woman rises
from the mound of wheat.

The woman cries with joy.
She gives
her torch
to a Guide and
the mother and daughter

embrace
tightly
in the relief of
having been reunited
after a long death.

Guides place honeyed
wheat cakes
into the mouths
of Seekers.

Guides: Be thou happy!
        Go, thou who art the goddesses'
        Faithfull followers.
        It is from the dead that food, growth and
        seeds
        come to us.
        Keep this divine secret in your hearts.
        You have nothing to fear.
        Through death, you will again bring Life.

The Seekers
Understand;
they now
Know.

Male
and
Female;
Slave

Free
they depart.

And their shining
beaming
faces
light the way back
to Athens.

What I Saw On the Train

I got on the train
somewhere in Brooklyn
and saw two people sitting together
at the end of the car.
Male and female
they sat
dressed in well-tailored black.
The man had a black beard and sidelocks.
She wore a scarf over her wig.
Every part of her was covered except
her hands and face—
her face was alarming.
She wore makeup like a painted clown.
Red lipstick smeared her lips.
Rouge had slapped her cheeks.
Bright blue eyeshadow had hit
her downcast eyes.
And my heart knew
what was happening.
He was displaying her face this way
in order to humiliate her.
Punishing her for some
"transgression".
Perhaps he had caught her
wearing just a touch of mascara
or a bit of powder
over slick skin.

She was being paraded in public
looking like Jezebel.
I wish I had gone up to them
and told her
You are beautiful.

*Your cheeks are adorned with ornaments
and on your body
hang the shields of warriors.
And the watchmen who punish you
are but scared little boys.*

With God or
without God;
with a man or
without a man
You are Beautiful.

The Caryatids of Macy's

Four maidens stand, supporting the weight
of Commerce, for that is their Fate.

Stone ribbons adorn stone sandals
as hordes below seek out sales.

Each holds the hand of another.
Plenty and hope are the alure

that entice the many below
to enter and peruse row after row

of clothing, jewels and pretty things—
while still voices can no longer sing

of freedom or of life and love.
They stand, supporting the weight above.

We Are All Hunters

We are all hunters in our own sweet way.
Some hunt for peace of mind; some hunt for time;
Some seek out Beauty; many spend their days
Searching for love. To hunt is not a crime---
For the world is a fierce place,
Though there are many who will still insist
They are too civilized for the Chase.
Who does not chase something? Wealth, joy or lost
Treasure---do not forget as you sit in
Offices and plant fields of Great Cost---
The wounds and the scars and the braying din;
The torn bodies and the ancient scent---
The gods of the hunter are Different.

Corinna Ties Her Hair

Corinna ties her hair in a ribbon
to celebrate her latest victory.
Let those men who only believe she won
due to vocal charms or a pretty knee
stew in their envy for another year.
This clear moment belongs solely to her.
Singing mountains and stories of nymph's cheer
and the old legends will one dark day blur
into mauled fragments of dry papyrus
to be judged by foreign scholars unknown,
who sit in small, closed spaces to discuss
the remains of her poems, down to the bone.
But for now, her triumph over Pindar
remains immune from scrutiny afar

Fragment

Someone, I tell you, will remember us---
even in another time, someone will
happen upon this artifact and thus
their heart will recognize us in the still
evening light. Some uncertain feeling must
rise from their heart to unwary mind, til
our raptures are recalled from age`ed hills.
The salt taste of your smooth and tanned skin, plus
the flavor of my lips will recombine
once more, despite every resting moment
between now and then. Someone will look back
and recall flesh on bone and cups of wine;
a time of passion not yet fully spent---
a time before we faded into Black.

Fourth of July

I failed to declare my independence
from independence---I lost that battle
at the end of a long, hot day, intense
with all the inane and idle prattle
of an obsessed brain, *Why doesn't he call?*
He said he would---why hasn't he, damn it?
His promise has become a cannonball
across the bow of my seemly spirit.
My heart cries, *to Hell with the Rules---call him!*
Who cares what others will think or say
about a lack of demureness so prim?
Make this night your own independence day
from those quaint, archaic, old world commands.
But I freeze, and then flounder for dry land.

For J. M.

Take my hand and follow me to the Edge---
where the land and the sea meet and mingle.
The moon awaits us, alone and single.
To hesitate would be a sacrilege.
Now's the time to act on what you allege---
that I make your brain and body tingle
throughout the long and remorseless day, dull
with your cares and worries---come to the ledge
with me, my love, and feel the deep, sharp thrill
of finally letting go and giving in.
Cling to me, take deep breaths, and then we'll JUMP.
At this point, for us, it is all downhill
anyway. Why delay much longer when
Ecstasy comes before the final Thump?

Before I Go Away for a Few Days

It's your own god-damned fault if I should die
and you, in cold shock, wallow in regret.
No explanations will then justify
your complete and utter failure to get
off your so fine ass and try to forget
that previous woman who burned your heart
and caused you to be so damned skittish---let
me be the antidote to her dark dart.
You have only to ask before we part
and I will be yours---my lips and my arms---
my breath and my blood await you to start
what you should have begun weeks ago---Harm
will not follow unless you fail to act
and let Fate take me, never to come back.

How the Fairytale Began

Good evening; the fairytale begins now.
In a secret forest full of monsters
our hero makes his way through dark green firs.
Misery and sweat hang from his broad brow
as he missteps into a place most foul.
He starts---and halts as his dim vision blurs.
He hears the snap of twigs—he endeavors
not to flee as he raises his taut bow.
His heart knows, though his mind is still unsure---
in just one moment he ceases to care
and lets fly an arrow . . . to hit a boar?
'Twas but a trifling; the mark 'twas but air---
Upon return, 'twill be a minotaur
and this bare spot of wood, it's horrid lair

How Greedy Am I

How greedy am I? You will soon find out---
your sole focus of being should be aimed
in my direction---of that, have no doubt.
All those strong, smooth muscles will be claimed
for my own and I will let no recall
from your past intrude upon our present.
Your heart beats in that well-structured chest wall
for my new adornment and amusement.
Your smile---I want that, too; it goes well
with my pearls. I want your attention,
your body, mind and every little cell.
Only this will tell me I have you won.
   And if we are luckier than the rest,
      how then, can you claim to be so oppressed?

About the author

Theresa Marie Reel lives in Harrisburg, Pennsylvania. This is a collection of poems written when she lived in Queens, NY. She would like to give a special thanks to the New Woodhaven Poetry Workshop and the Gotham Writers Workshop. She has written several volumes of poetry: Dove Season, Daydream/Nightmare, Defective Hearts and Dim is the Light. She has also written a fantasy/romance novel titled "Warlock Love". She can be contacted at reeltheresa@hotmai.com.

Made in the USA
Middletown, DE
10 March 2023

26345529R00033